MW00715418

Let Your Light
SHINE

A Memoir of Betrayal and God's Healing

Katherine J. Winters

LET YOUR LIGHT SHINE
Copyright © 2016 by Katherine J. Winters

All rights reserved. Neither this publication nor any part of this publication may be reproduced or transmitted in any form or by any means, electronic or mechanical, including photocopying, recording or any information storage and retrieval system, without permission in writing from the author.

Unless otherwise indicated, all Scripture quotations are taken from the New King James Version®. Copyright © 1982 by Thomas Nelson. Used by permission. All rights reserved. • Scripture quotations marked AMP are taken from the Amplified® Bible. Copyright © 2015 by The Lockman Foundation, La Habra, CA 90631. All rights reserved. • Scripture quotations marked GNT are from the Good News Translation® (Today's English Version, Second Edition) Copyright © 1992 American Bible Society. All rights reserved.

Printed in Canada

ISBN: 978-1-4866-1350-2

Word Alive Press
131 Cordite Road, Winnipeg, MB R3W 1S1
www.wordalivepress.ca

Library and Archives Canada Cataloguing in Publication

Winters, Katherine J., 1955-, author
        Let your light shine : a memoir of betrayal and God's healing / Katherine J. Winters.

Issued in print and electronic formats.
ISBN   978-1-4866-1350-2   (paperback).--ISBN   978-1-4866-1351-9 (ebook)

        1. Winters, Katherine J., 1955-. 2. Christian women--Biography. 3. Christian biography. I. Title.

BV4527.W562 2016   270.092   C2016-903621-9
                                                             C2016-903622-7

CONTENTS

ACKNOWLEDGEMENTS

To my Nana, who passed away in 1998, for her faith, spiritual courage, and inner strength to go through the legal challenge for guardianship of my siblings and me in 1963. Nana gave us her best in providing a better life and removing us from the unspeakable horrors of childhood abuse.

To Pat Hamill, for her friendship, her faith, and her compassion, which helped me to unlock the doors of my past and its emotional pain. God's love and her spiritual counselling gave me the courage and inner strength to continue on this journey of healing. Pat is truly one of God's missionaries. She draws people to the love of God through love and compassion. Pat has become my very dear friend and mentor. She came into my life a few years after my Nana passed away, when I felt very lonely and lost emotionally. I had a spiritual connection with Pat that I had not experienced with any other person. She understood where I was coming from emotionally, and she took me into her heart and into her open and very loving arms just like a mother would do. I've been able to phone her during difficult times, and she has prayed for me and prayed with me and has held me in her arms and allowed me to shed the tears of anguish that were locked deep in my soul for so many years.

To Rita Wold, who was first an acquaintance and then became my friend, accepting me where I was emotionally, for holding me in her arms and allowing me to cry when I needed to most, and also for her spiritual wisdom during my counselling sessions on my journey of healing. Thank you for sharing your gift of music with me; you've touched my heart and soul many times through the hymns that you've played.

To Janie Loney, for her friendship, faith, spiritual counselling, and emotional support, which were able to unlock the door of my past when I asked Jesus to come into my heart and do a cleaning and healing in the areas of my life that were affected by the abuse I endured as a child. And for her time and her patience in working with me on this project that God placed on my heart ten years ago, which is allowing me to give my testimony to those who are still experiencing the trauma of sexual abuse in their lives.

INTRODUCTION

For it is shameful even to speak of those things which are done by them in secret. But all things that are exposed are made manifest by the light, for whatever makes manifest is light. Therefore He says: "Awake, you who sleep, Arise from the dead, And Christ will give you light." (Ephesians 5:12–14)

I've always known I had a secret, a secret so devastating to my soul that I couldn't acknowledge it. Intense shame kept me from accepting the truth of this secret.

Even at a very young age, as an infant in diapers, I knew instinctively that I couldn't trust certain adults in my life. It would be years before I would come to understand that chaos, trauma, abuse, and severe neglect should not be the norm in a child's life; in fact, they're abnormal.

In the first five years of my life I underwent numerous surgeries to correct rectal damage from the extreme abuse.

Sexual abuse was suspected, but to my knowledge no one investigated.

There were certain adults in my life whom I couldn't trust, no matter how much I was groomed to trust them. I wanted to trust them, but I knew in my heart that I couldn't. Something was wrong.

This secret left my soul empty to the core, and my heart ached for a love from my parents that simply wasn't there. All my life I had been searching for answers to this secret, that I might be released from the hell that my soul was enduring. This was an indescribable hell that gripped me with such fear that I couldn't allow myself to trust anyone, for the two people that I was groomed to trust had betrayed me from day one of my life, leaving me desolate, with an intense shame and fear that no one else could see or feel. And no one could enter in.

I always had feelings that something bad had happened to me as a child. At times when I experienced an emotional trigger it was like I was watching a slow-motion movie of the trauma that I suffered. Yes, I've always known that I had a terrible secret, but it would be years before I would have the inner courage and spiritual strength to investigate the horrific secret that I carried so deeply in my soul. The flashbacks got worse over time, as did the nightmares. I knew I had to investigate what happened to me as a child and why it happened.

CHILD SEXUAL ABUSE WARNING SIGNS
(Parents Protect!, accessed March 30, 2016, www. parentsprotect.co.uk/warning_signs.htm)

Children often show us rather than tell us that something is upsetting them. There may be many reasons for changes in their behaviour, but if we notice a combination of worrying signs it may be time to call for help or advice.

What to watch out for in children:
- Acting out in an inappropriate sexual way with toys or objects
- Nightmares, sleeping problems
- Becoming withdrawn or very clingy
- Becoming unusually secretive
- Sudden unexplained personality changes, mood swings and seeming insecure
- Regressing to younger behaviours, e.g. bedwetting
- Unaccountable fear of particular places or people
- Outburst of anger
- Changes in eating habits
- New adult words for body parts and no obvious source
- Talk of a new, older friend and unexplained money or gifts
- Self-harm (cutting, burning or other harmful activities)

- Physical signs, such as, unexplained soreness or bruises around genitals or mouth, sexually transmitted diseases, pregnancy
- Running away
- Not wanting to be alone with a particular child or young person

Any one sign doesn't mean that a child was or is being sexually abused, but the presence of several suggests that you should begin to ask questions and consider seeking help. Keep in mind that some of these signs can emerge at other times of stress such as:

- During a divorce
- Death of a family member or pet
- Problems at school or with friends
- Other anxiety-inducing or traumatic events

Physical warning signs

Physical signs of sexual abuse are rare, however, if you see these signs, take your child to a doctor. Your doctor can help you understand what may be happening and test for sexually transmitted diseases.

- Pain, discoloration, bleeding or discharges in genitals, anus or mouth
- Persistent or recurring pain during urination and bowel movements
- Wetting and soiling accidents unrelated to toilet training

One

GUARDIANSHIP

Although my father and my mother have abandoned me,
Yet the LORD will take me up [adopt me as His child].
(Psalm 27:10 AMP)

I was born into a family of extreme dysfunction. My father was an alcoholic, and my mother didn't have natural mothering instincts. In fact, my parents were both quite rebellious in many ways and irresponsible.

In 1963 my grandmother was granted guardianship for my brother, Rick (one year older than me), my sister, Lee (one year younger than me), and me, and we went to live with Nana. It was a huge change. I didn't understand what was happening or why we couldn't live with Mom and Dad anymore. Nana would get very irritated and at times angry if we asked her why we were living with her. She'd say, "It has to be this way" or "You're too young to understand. Don't ask me anymore about it."

Nana gave my sister and me a room to share, which was great. My brother had his own room. It took a while for us to adjust to a new life and new routines. The first few months were very turbulent as we adjusted to Nana's strict and very protective manner. We'd argue with her, but we soon learned the rules of her house and what was acceptable and what wasn't.

We had to go to a new school, which meant making new friends and meeting new teachers. That feeling of having a secret kept popping up in my gut, but I wasn't able to tell anyone about it. Living with Nana didn't take away the very deep shame I walked in.

Nana made sure we had warm beds to sleep in with sheets, blankets, and pillows; comfortable clothes to wear for the different seasons, including boots to keep our feet warm in the winter; enough food to eat; and regular baths, which included getting our hair washed. She also taught us to say bedtime prayers, which we didn't do at Mom and Dad's. And most importantly, when I woke up in the middle of the night at Nana's, Dad or his drinking buddies weren't passed out in my bed, sleeping next to me. My siblings and I saw Mom and Dad on the weekends for court-ordered unsupervised visits.

Looking back at that period in time, I now realize that had it not been for Nana's courage to go through a legal challenge to gain custody of us, we might have died in childhood from the severe abuse and the extreme trauma that we were forced to endure. No one else seemed to care. Thank you, Nana.

My siblings and I were treated like the black sheep of the family because of Mom and Dad's excessive drinking. I really don't remember a time when they weren't drunk. That was normal to me. Sometimes they would start drinking early in the day; it depended on how early in the day Dad's drinking buddies came to see him. They usually brought a couple of cases of beer, which they consumed over the course of the day. As the visiting got underway and stories were told, the beer would really start to flow. Then Mom and Dad would start arguing, getting louder and more vulgar. The drunker they got, the louder and more vulgar they became, especially Dad.

I remember hating to have to go to see my parents when we were living at Nana's. The three of us usually alternated in visiting them on weekends. There was seldom enough to eat; the fridge and the cupboards were usually empty. Nana, who was uncomfortable with the terms of the court order, would pop in unexpectedly, bringing extra food, extra blankets, or even extra clothes for us kids. When the weekend visit was over we would then go back to Nana's place and be in a safe and strict environment again.

Oftentimes there would be very heated arguments between Nana and Mom and Dad on the phone about what had taken place during the visitation that weekend, and that's when I saw Nana's ugly side, which frightened me. Her anger spilled over onto us children inappropriately many times, in the form of a severe spanking because we had dared to say "No." She would yell at us, "You'll do as you're told or I'll send you back to the squalor that I just took you from." Then she would send one of us to our room for the rest of the day.

This weekly transition was always difficult. Going from Mom and Dad's place back to Nana's was like going from dark to light, from chaos and confusion to structure and safety. And now I see that life with Nana wasn't always safe either. We saw flares of her rage especially when for some unknown reason Mom or Dad failed to show up for a planned weekend or called at the last minute to cancel.

A couple of years after we started living with Nana, I was injured in a tobogganing accident. I don't remember much of the accident except having a lot of fun going down a hill covered with snow. Then something hit me from behind. I woke up sometime later in hospital. My spine had been injured, affecting my right leg.

I lived with Nana for eleven years. She did her best to give us a structured environment and more than just the basics of what every child needs and deserves. But I also remember running away from Nana's place many times because of the arguing between Mom, Dad, and Nana. I always felt like a piece of property that was about to be divided up between the adults, especially when they were arguing about the weekend visits or the holidays and where us kids were to go for that day or period of time.

Then there were the fun times when Nana invited her lady friends to visit and they'd bring their children. When my sister and I knew that they were coming over, we'd plan a tea party, which included special sandwiches, juice, and a few cookies. My sister and I got dressed up in our play clothes (play dresses that Nana had given us) with fancy hats and a touch of lipstick. That was fun.

I remember Nana going to a lot of work to make birthdays fun. They included a craft, making our own party hats from construction paper of various colours, glue, crayons, and sparkles. She also did her best to make Christmases and other holidays a special time for us.

We made homemade ice cream many times. Boy, that was fun! Nana used farm fresh cream, ice, salt, and a couple of other ingredients. She would cook the mixture on the stove, let it cool slightly, then pour it into a metal canister that sat in the middle of a wooden bucket. Then she poured ice cubes around the metal canister and some salt onto the ice cubes. She fastened the metal canister into place in the centre of the wooden bucket. My siblings and I and our friends would take turns cranking the handle on the ice cream maker until the ice cream was made. What a memorable time and delicious treat!

I remember Nana buying a playhouse for us. She put it in the backyard, at the edge of the lawn. It was eight by ten feet, mainly white, with two windows to the right of the door. The windows had screens on them to keep the bugs out and red and white shutters on the front that we could close when it rained. Oh how I loved that playhouse! We added a single bed and a small bookshelf that held a set of dishes for when we had snacks. Nana gave us a small lamp that we used when we needed to. We had a small table that would seat two people; we could fold it up if we needed extra space. We also had two folding chairs. We had a lot of fun in that playhouse. Many times during the summer months my sister and I even slept in there. We could close the shutters and lock the door to feel safe.

Nana also got us a teeter-totter. It was made from a huge industrial wire spool that we put a big plank on. It had two wooden wheels on it, one on either end, and we placed cement bricks beside each one to keep it in place while we were playing on it. We could move the teeter-totter anywhere in the yard if we wanted to. We just lifted the plank off the spool, removed the cement bricks that kept the wheels in place, then rolled the spool to a new location. We had a lot of fun on that teeter-totter.

Nana planted a garden every spring. She grew carrots, peas, lettuce, tomatoes, radishes, green onions, parsley, and potatoes.

One Christmas Nana made pull taffy. That was fabulous fun! She gathered all the ingredients, cooked it on the stove, then let it cool for a bit so that we wouldn't get burned. Nana always made sure that the taffy had cooled enough to handle before she gave it to us to pull. She made sure that we washed our hands well. Then she put a bit of butter on our hands and told us to rub it around in our palms. The butter kept the taffy from sticking to us. Listening to her directions, we thought this was a funny thing to do. Nana then put us in teams of two and told us to pull and twist the taffy as it cooled. By the time we were done with the pull taffy that night we'd had a lot of fun and we'd made a yummy treat that we could eat.

Nana really made learning fun. She would tell us stories while we did activities. Then at the end she'd ask what we had learned from the story and the activity.

There were times when the holidays seemed to go really fast. Then before we knew it we'd be getting ready to go back to school and settling into our structured routine, which included doing our homework, helping Nana with various tasks around the house, getting together with our friends on weekends once our studies were done, and going to church on Sundays.

Nana told my siblings and about Jesus and just how much Jesus loves us and that He died on the cross for our sins (John 3:16). I was eight years old when I accepted Jesus into my heart. I think I did this mostly to please Nana.

A few times when I was back at Nana's after a weekend at Mom and Dad's, after I had a bath, put on my pyjamas, had a snack, and went to bed, I woke up a few hours later from a terrible nightmare. It was usually the same: I was fighting off men who were raping me. I'd be crying, screaming, and kicking, trying desperately to fight these men off. Nana would gently wake me up. Then she would wrap me in a blanket, hold me on her knees, and rock me to sleep in her rocking chair, singing Christian songs like "Jesus Loves Me" and "He's Got the Whole World in His Hands."

As I got older I kept praying that Jesus would help Mom and Dad to stop drinking because of all the emotional, physical, mental, and sexual trauma that my brother, sister, and I endured. As time moved forward my siblings and I continued in our daily schedules of school, church, and various other activities. As I've said, however, I came to dread the weekends. It meant that one of us three kids had to see Mom and Dad.

I managed to get through school, but it was very difficult. For me school was an escape from the chaos that was going on in my life, especially with Mom and Dad. There were times when I simply could not retain the information I was studying. Regardless of how many times I read and reread it, I couldn't grasp or retain the information.

When I was in grade 7, I collapsed in school. I remember doing a spelling test in the morning. Later that morning the teacher was giving the test results to the students. As he placed the paper on my desk I experienced an intense flashback of abuse at the hands of my father. Why this flashback surfaced at that time, I have no idea.

I could hardly find my way out of the classroom, but I knew I had to escape. I crawled out the door to a corner in the hallway, huddled up into a ball, and wept. An intense thought kept hitting me: *I can't let Daddy rape me again.* I couldn't explain to anyone what I was feeling in that moment. I knew that the principal and teachers—the adults in authority—wouldn't understand. How could I tell them that I had been repeatedly raped by my own father and that, when he was done, his drinking buddies took their turns? And when I fought to stop them I was either choked or drugged into submission. These men took what they wanted sexually from me; they didn't care how I felt about it. I had fragmented into many pieces in my soul just to survive the repeated assaults by them.

I don't remember much after that hellish experience at school. I woke up some time later in hospital, where I stayed for about a week. Thinking back, I remember I slept a lot during that time. When I was released to go home I was given a mild sedative daily to sleep. Nana was adamant that I not say anything to anyone about this. She made it very clear to me that no one would believe me anyway. I was told not to talk anyone about why I was in hospital or why I collapsed in school.

I don't remember if I finished the school year or not. I did, however, get my report card, saying that I had passed into the next grade.

Grade 8 was a better year for me. I was placed in a special education program for children with learning disabilities. It took me a while to adjust to my studies, but I didn't find my classes as hard to understand from then on.

By the time I was in grade 10 I knew in my gut that as soon as I finished my education and graduated I had to leave. I desperately wanted to leave Winnipeg. I realized that I was going to have to move from this community of nightmares. After visiting my parents for possibly the last time I knew that I must take this step for my life and future.

So I got through my studies and graduated from grade 11 (there was no grade 12 in this special program), and a few months later I found a job working nights as a nurse aide in a seniors' lodge. I had graduated in June, and by September I was working full time.

I continued to live at Nana's for a while longer, but after a few months I realized that I wanted to live on my own. It was becoming more difficult to talk with Nana as time went on. She wanted me to spend more time with her on my days off. She was also starting to tell me who I could and could not see as far as dating. Yes, I was starting to date, which Nana really didn't like at all. She told me a few times in not so nice words that all boys ever want from a girl is sex; once they get that from you, they don't care about you anymore. "The boys will drop you like a dirty shirt." I found that comment to be very rude. She was becoming very critical of some of my friendships, which I didn't appreciate.

My co-workers and the residents at the lodge were looking forward to the holiday season. I was just glad to be working. I really wasn't giving Christmas much thought that year. I was thinking more about the move that I was planning on making at some point in the future and the money that I still needed to save in order to make that move. During this holiday season I was anticipating spending some time with Nana and getting together with friends I hadn't seen in a while.

Before I knew it Christmas had arrived, and the holiday celebrations were underway. Spending time with Nana was causing me to feel a little apprehensive, as I really didn't want to discuss any of my friendships with her at this time; that discussion would be at a later date. I wanted to enjoy this holiday season without arguing with her. Then there were get-togethers with family and friends. Incidentally, these did not include Mom and Dad.

Life slowed down again for a bit after the holidays, and aside from working, which I thoroughly enjoyed, I was contemplating the move I was planning.

By early spring I had been working at the lodge for about six months, and I knew it was time to take wing. I wasn't sure at the time just where I would move to, but I knew that I needed to leave Nana's place.

I had met a new friend a few months before, and when I got to know her better I mentioned to her that I wanted to move out from Nana's nest. She said that she was looking for a roommate and asked if I would be interested. I told her I'd get back to her in a couple of days with an answer.

On my day off from work, I was spending time with Nana. We were sitting at her kitchen table talking, and I told her about my plans to move. Boy, did she ever become furious! It was one of the few times when Nana's anger actually scared me. I couldn't believe that she got so angry with me. I left the kitchen quickly and went up the stairs to my room on the second floor. I knew in that moment that I was moving in with my friend Kathy. However, this was not the way I wanted the move to go. I packed a few things in a suitcase and proceeded down the stairs just as quickly.

I was trying to be mature about this decision, and I told Nana that I would be back later to pick up the rest of my things. I left her house shaking like a leaf. I couldn't believe that Nana had just yelled at me like that. I managed, with that heavy suitcase and poor balance, to make my way down the street to a pay phone, and I called Kathy. Boy, was I relieved when she answered! I told her what had just taken place between Nana and me and asked if I could move in immediately. Thankfully she agreed, and she said she would pick me up shortly right at that pay phone.

It didn't take long before I was settled in at Kathy's place, which was now my new home. I had my own room, and we agreed on sharing the common expenses. I was also glad that

I was working full time and that I could get back to work the next day, as it took my mind off of the way that Nana had reacted with such anger.

I really wanted to connect with my grandmother, but it was a couple of months before I was able to make that connection. I was busy with work, and the few times that I tried to reach her on the phone, there was no answer. I did eventually reach her, and I asked if I could come over to visit. I apologized to her and told her that I never meant to shock her or upset her. I was eighteen years old, and the combination of Nana's demands and my growing sense of independence made it very difficult for me to continue living with her. It was just time for me to move out from Nana's nest. I also made it very clear to her that I would not be moving back home. I think she must have understand somewhat, in spite of her own needs and plans regarding me. At least we didn't argue this time. I left that visit in peace.

Summer was quickly approaching. I couldn't believe how fast time was flying. It was now a couple of months since I had moved in with Kathy. All was well. Life went on.

A cousin, Marney, lived near Edmonton. One evening I phoned her and told her what had been happening in my life. I also mentioned that I wanted to get away for a couple of days, maybe even a weekend. She asked me if I'd like to come to Edmonton for a visit. She said that the summer holidays or Christmas might be a good time. Her invitation was tempting, and I told her that I would get back to her. The more I thought about this opportunity, the more excited I got, but I felt that I might not be able to put enough extra money aside before summer. I decided that taking my holidays later, at Christmas, would work better for me. I looked forward to that trip down the road.

Summer was upon us. The weather was warm, and the noonday sun shining on me made me feel great. I loved to spend time outside.

I kept busy with work, and it was going well for me. I loved working at the lodge, even though I didn't interact much with the residents, mostly because I worked the night shift. However, if a resident buzzed the nurses' desk and required help, then I would respond with assistance. They might ask to get their water jug refreshed, or sometimes their walker had been moved after they had gone to bed and they needed it to be placed by their bedside. I had come to know a few more of the staff at the lodge, who were great people to work with. I was teamed up with another nurse aide, and we worked well together.

I remember one Christmas when we waited all day at Nana's for Mom and Dad to show up to celebrate Christmas with us. When my siblings and I weren't busy helping Nana with Christmas dinner, I sat at the top of the stairs, waiting for them to either show up or call to say that they were going to be late. They didn't call, and they didn't show up. I realized then that

Mom and Dad's excessive drinking and deviant lifestyle had destroyed any hope of us ever being a family again. It had been a family of horrendous—even terrifying—dysfunction.

I knew I had to leave the province. I really didn't want to move away, but I felt compelled in my spirit. I was having flashbacks of the abuse that just wouldn't go away, flashbacks that came and went throughout my teen years, and I knew I had to flee from this toxic memory. And I had learned through the years that Nana was the only person whom I could truly count on or trust. Even in her imperfections, I trusted her. My siblings and I had been hurt enough by our parents' drinking. Besides, now I was of legal age to leave. I didn't need anyone's permission to move away from home. So many special events had come and gone without Mom and Dad being there for them, physically or emotionally. It was time for me to move forward with my life.

The year passed quickly, and before I knew it, the Christmas holidays had arrived, and I made my trip to Edmonton. During that visit I decided that I was going to move to Alberta in the spring. I knew when I got back to Winnipeg after Christmas that I would indeed be moving. I did, however, need to continue working for a few more months to save the money necessary to make the move possible. I was getting excited at the thought of this move becoming a reality for me.

CHILD SEXUAL ABUSE IN CANADA
(SexAssault.ca, accessed March 30, 2016, http://
www.sexassault.ca/childabuse.htm)

Child sexual abuse is one of the most misunderstood and underreported crimes in Canada. Most commonly the perpetrators of sexual abuse against children are not strangers, but those closest to the child. This includes family members, mentors, priests, teachers, etc. Because these abusers are in a position of trust toward the child, they have both the opportunity to abuse and are able to convince the child that:

   a) the behaviour is okay or normal
   b) not to report the behaviour (by using either threats or promises)
   c) if the child reports the behaviour they will not be believed

The relationship of influence and trust is the #1 reason child abuse is rarely reported…If you suspect a loved one is being sexually abused and/or you recognized some or many of the above noted warning signs, it's time to act now.

Steps to Take
The appropriate action to take depends on your relation to the child. If you are a third party that is aware of a child being sexually abused, you ought to report it

to the local Children's Aid Society in your province/county.

If you are the parent or guardian of a child who reports, or you suspects, is being sexually abused, it is crucial that you facilitate honest and open discussion with the child about exactly what happened. To do this effectively the child must feel comfortable in talking to you. Usually the most important thing you can do to make the child feel comfortable is to ensure the child that you believe what they are telling you (especially considering the child may have been told by their abuser that nobody would believe them). It is also crucial that you do not place blame on the child for the abuse. Remember not to place blame by asking questions that suggest fault on the part of the child, such as: "why didn't you tell me earlier?"

The next step is usually to contact a health professional (medical doctor) to collect evidence and perform needed health tests (such as checking for STDs and other trauma/infections). Do not wash or bath the child before such medical examinations as this may destroy evidence. Depending on the circumstances, and the province you are in, the doctor may also have a positive duty to report the abuse to the local Children's Aid Society for an investigation. The doctor may suggest the child see a mental health professional, or you as a parents, may decide it is beneficial to the child's recovery.

While we recognize that reporting sexual abuse to the police can be a traumatic experience for victims, we encourage reporting the crime to the police immediately (other children may be in significant danger).

DUTY TO REPORT

(*Education Canada*, September 2015, accessed March 30, 2016, http://www.cea-ace.ca/education-canada/article/duty-report)

What every teacher should know about reporting child abuse

Teachers are in a unique position to notice that child abuse may be occurring due to the extensive amount of time that they spend with their students. Yet teachers are often not adequately prepared by their school boards on issues relating to detecting and reporting child abuse. This article provides essential information regarding a teacher's duty to report children in need of protection, including: when teachers are required to report child abuse, common legal questions, signs and indicators of abuse, how to respond to disclosures of abuse, how to make a report, and what happens after a report is made. Teachers should also refer to their board's specific policy on reporting children in need of protection. If you suspect that a child might be in need of protection, contact your local Children's Aid Society.

The requirement to report

Everyone is legally required to report when they suspect child abuse has occurred. No province or territory requires the person who suspects abuse to collect evidence to support their claim...

Keeping records

Keep a journal that contains observations of your students, including observations of unusual behaviour or worrisome physical symptoms. Keeping records serves two purposes. First, your notes over time may provide enough information to warrant you to suspect that a child may be in need of protection. Second, this information can be subpoenaed in court if a case arises. Therefore, records must only contain facts, observations, and direct conversations with the child. In addition, each entry should be dated and signed.

What if you are unsure?

If you are unsure that abuse has occurred, you have three options:

1. Consult colleagues. Get support and advice from your colleagues and supervisors. Compare notes and brainstorm possible strategies.

2. Call the local Children's Aid Society. An intake worker at the Society will listen to your concerns. At this point you do not have to provide your name or the name of the child. The intake worker will let you know if your concerns warrant opening a case. If the intake worker believes there is suspected abuse, you will be asked to provide identifying information on the child and yourself.

3. Speak with the child. Use open-ended questions, for instance, "How did you get that bruise?" It is critical that you do not use leading questions or probe for answers. Child abuse cases can be dismissed in court if it is felt that the initial interviewers biased the children. Be aware that asking questions may result in the child disclosing abuse has occurred.

When a child discloses

It is essential for teachers to understand how to properly respond to students who have disclosed they were abused. If a student discloses abuse to you:

Stay calm and listen. Let the child tell his or her story. The child needs to know that it is okay to talk about what happened. If a disclosure is made during class time, have someone relieve you of your class duties so that you can continue talking with the student privately.

Go slowly. Let the child tell you what happened in his or her own way. Record what the child says verbatim. Do not adjust the child's use of language.

Be supportive. Let children who confide in you know that:

- They are not in trouble and have not done anything wrong;
- You believe them and they did the right thing by telling you;
- They are not to blame for what happened;
- You will do everything you can to help;
- You know other people who can help them.

Don't probe for details. It is sufficient to get only general information or the basic facts. The child will have to tell his or her story to a child protection worker, and potentially the police.

Explain to the child what will happen next. Let the child know you will need to report the abuse or neglect, and that you will be talking to a child protection worker who may need to come and talk to the child.

Be honest. If the child asks questions, answer what you can. If you do not know the answer, it's okay to say, "I don't know."

Do not make promises you cannot keep. Don't promise to keep the abuse or neglect a secret.

How to report suspected abuse

1. Make notes; date and sign your entry.
2. Locate your school board's policy or procedure on reporting suspected child abuse. Some boards have reports that must be filled out when a call is made to a Children's Aid Society.
3. Inform your principal that you will be making a report. If the principal is not available, continue on with the reporting process and contact the principal as soon as reasonably possible.
4. Call the local Children's Aid Society. You will need to provide the following information to the intake worker:

- Child's name, age, gender, address, and names and ages of any siblings who live with the child;
- Parent's name and address;
- Nature and extent of the injury or condition observed;
- Prior injuries/suspicions and when observed;
- Actions taken by the reporter (e.g. talking with the child);
- Where the act occurred;
- Your name, location, and contact information (your name will not be given to the parents; however, the caseworker will say the report came from the child's school).

There are also questions you should ask the intake worker:

- If a case will be opened;
- If someone will be coming to the school to interview the child;
- Who is responsible for contacting the parents;
- When updates on the case will be provided;
- Any other questions you may have.

Two

SECRETS

For the word of God is living and powerful, and sharper than any two-edged sword, piercing even to the division of soul and spirit, and of joints and marrow, and is a discerner of the thoughts and intents of the heart. And there is no creature hidden from His sight, but all things are naked and open to the eyes of Him to whom we must give account. (Hebrews 4:12–13)

I naively thought that moving to a new province would mean a whole new life. I was sadly mistaken. Secrets became a way of life for me. No one could find out the truth about the abuse I experienced as a child or the nightmares that continued to plague me.

I was constantly very aware of my painful past. I saw that I was consistently keeping people at arm's length. Why?

I didn't want people to know about the abuse. There's a stigma attached to issues of abuse, especially when you have been sexually abused. If you're physically abused, there are generally bruises or cuts on your body to prove that you've been hurt. But when you're sexually abused, that's a whole other issue. You just don't talk about it. It happens behind closed doors.

There's an issue of trust when you meet someone for the first time. You either trust them or you don't. You learn to trust your gut instinct.

Deep shame held me in chains, and I had no clue how to unlock them. I felt empty inside. Oh sure, I had physically moved away from home, from the past, and was gradually building a new life, but that wasn't fixing the problem.

I was in my late teens, which brought new adventures and experiences, but I still couldn't escape. Every time I met someone new, a protective wall came up, not allowing me to make friends. Terror would hit me and that invisible wall would go up.

I stayed with my cousin Marney and her family when I first moved to Alberta. I applied for jobs at various businesses that were looking to hire people with my qualifications, and it wasn't long before I got a phone call about a job interview. I was thrilled at first, but then I became nervous. I knew, however, that I had most of the skills required for the job posted.

Being qualified for a job and being hired weren't the problems. I was anxious about the questions that were about to come about my personal life, like how long had I been living in Edmonton and what brought me to Edmonton in the first place. Did I have family? Oh dear, what else might they ask me?

For most people these questions wouldn't pose a problem, but for me this was a huge concern. Nobody could know what I experienced or endured in my life and family. I just wanted to put a lid on my past, forget it, and leave it there.

Well, I got the job and was delighted. For a couple of months my cousin drove me back and forth from the suburbs of Edmonton to my job. Later on I moved into a suite close to work, which made life a whole lot easier. I didn't always need to be asking family for a ride, but I still got together with them when I wasn't working.

I held my job, in a nursing home, for about a year. Then my right leg started to bother me a lot, which made it difficult for me to be on my feet for long periods of time. My balance was being affected by that tobogganing injury of years ago, and I realized that I was going to have to give up that job.

I had made friends with many of the seniors in the nursing home. They told me about their growing up years, the families they came from, and the hobbies they enjoyed. I thoroughly enjoyed my relationship with these dear old folks. The focus was never on me, so when I decided I needed to address this old tobogganing injury, it was with a heavy heart.

I took physiotherapy for a few months and used the time of transition to refocus on the type of job that I would be able to do. I really wasn't interested in dating, but I met my husband-to-be during this time.

Earlier in Edmonton I had dated a young man for a brief period and even got engaged to him. This was a short-lived and bad relationship. He had character flaws that reminded me of the trauma I had been through as a child. My perspective of male-female interaction and relationship development was so jaded that I believed that men generally expected to be in bed with a girl after the second or third date. And that's why I was not interested in dating, period!

Allan and I met at a church social in November 1975. His eyes and his incredible smile captured my heart. He made me laugh, and he had a clean spirit about him. He was in town visiting his family and would soon be heading back up north to work driving a truck. He asked if he could phone me when he came back to Edmonton. I gave him my phone number, but I didn't really expect him to call me. But the next time he was back in town, he called. I was surprised and excited all at the same time. We got together for a coffee, and again I thoroughly enjoyed our time.

A few months later, Allan called me again and told me that he had moved to Edmonton. I was surprised and thrilled. There was an invitation to visit and spend time together, and the relationship continued.

We became real friends. I loved his company and his clean sense of humour.

As time went on I knew in my heart that I needed to share my secret with this incredible man. I needed him to hear that I had been molested as a child. I felt I had to be open and honest with him because he had captured my heart and soul. But I really had no clue at this point as to the extent of the abuse I had endured as a child. When the trauma is so severe, the victim's mind and body have a way of blocking out the worst of it so that he or she can survive. It wasn't until years later, when through counselling I investigated the truth of the abuse and the body memories and flashbacks, that I came to understand the extent of the abuse.

We continued to enjoy one another's friendship for a couple of years. Allan gradually introduced to me to his family. He had an older sister, Emily, who lived in Calgary, and we drove there to visit for a weekend getaway. Boy, was I nervous! I wasn't sure what to expect, but it was a great weekend.

Emily was a married mother of four children and had a very caring nature about her. It felt strange at first to watch how they interacted as a family, but I felt safe with them.

The weekend visit drew to a close, and Allan and I prepared to head back to Edmonton, planning to come back to see Emily and her family on the next long weekend. As we were driving home we talked about the visit, and I told Allan how much I enjoyed getting to know Emily and her family. I also said that I was starting to feel restless about where I was living and at times felt like I needed to move from Edmonton.

Allan asked me if I would be interested in moving to Calgary. I said sure; there really wasn't anything holding me in Edmonton. Then I asked Allan about his job, as he seemed to be enjoying his work. He said he wanted to study to get his mechanic's licence and could do that in Calgary.

I wondered where would we live if we moved to Calgary. Allan said that maybe we would stay with his sister. So went our conversation.

When we got back home to Edmonton he continued with his work and I continued with my physio and work search.

It wasn't long before the May long weekend arrived and we returned to visit the family in Calgary. During this visit Allan told his sister that we planned to move to Calgary and that he would get his mechanic's licence and I would look for work.

To our pleasure, before long our move to Calgary was in motion, and Emily was gracious to give us accommodations until we could make it on our own. Allan applied and was accepted to study for a mechanic's licence, and I went to work in a seniors' lodge. After six months I had saved enough money to rent an apartment of my own, and Allan continued to board with his sister.

I started to really miss Nana. We called each other about once a week, and I loved those phone calls. Hearing her voice always brightened my day. To me Nana's voice was like a beacon in the dark.

I eventually asked her if she would like to move to Calgary to live with me. Not long after, she did in fact move in with me. We rented a two-bedroom apartment, and it was great having her with me.

I loved my life, going to work every day, having my own apartment, but there were still times when I struggled with the fact that I had been molested when I was a young child. The torment didn't go away, and I still found it very difficult to make friends. Anytime I met someone new, that invisible wall would go up again. I had to keep people at arm's length, and I hated that feeling.

As Allan and I settled into a new community, we enjoyed our friendship, and we made friends through his work and mine. We occasionally talked about getting married. I knew I loved him with all my heart, so I asked him to marry me. That's right, *I* asked *him* to marry me! I knew I was ready for marriage, and I knew Allan was the man I wanted to spend the rest of my life with. He gave a resounding yes! Not long after that, we got engaged. I was thrilled to pieces.

Over the course of the next year Allan introduced me to the rest of his siblings. Each time, as I prepared to meet another member of his family, that invisible protective wall came up. I hated that response in me; it left me feeling very lonely and isolated. Nevertheless, his family accepted me with open arms. For sure it took me some time to adjust to the way his family came together for celebrations, whether it was a birthday or another occasion. I wasn't used to the way a healthy family interacts.

EFFECTS OF ABUSE

(ASCA, Adults Surviving Childhood Abuse, accessed March 30, 2016, http://www.asca.org.au/WHAT-WE-DO/For-Survivors/Resources-for-Survivors/How-can-abuse-affect-me)

Experiencing any form of childhood trauma and abuse can impact on an adult's quality of life in fundamental ways. It can make basic day-to-day activities, such as eating, sleeping, working and study difficult. Trauma and abuse in childhood can also affect your mental health, physical health, and your relationships with the people around you.

However research has established that recovery is possible. With the right help and support survivors can live healthy connected lives. Understanding the effects of trauma and abuse can help survivors connect their past experiences with their present challenges, and find pathways to a healthier future.

Effects on Feelings

Survivors are often out of touch with their feelings—confused by emotions or reactions they cannot explain. They have often been raised in environments in which a child's normal expressions of upset or discomfort were punished or ignored. They may have been taught to attribute the negative emotions associated with childhood trauma and abuse, such as shame and anger, towards themselves. This confusion often persists into adult life, and can result in heightened experiences of:

- Anxiety
- Grief and sadness
- Shame, self blame and guilt
- Alienation
- Helplessness, hopelessness and powerlessness

Like everyone, survivors have a right to "a life worth living" (Linehan 1993), but instead survivors often live with chronic distress and pain. For many survivors, these emotions are so much a part of their day-to-day life that they don't realise that there are alternatives. Unable to readily regulate their emotions they may seek to do so through alcohol, drugs, sex, gambling, or other compulsive behaviours. Many survivors also harm themselves out of a sense of despair. All of these *'coping strat*egies' make sense in the context of childhood trauma and abuse.

Learning about emotions—what they are, where they come from, and how to respond to them—is a crucial part of finding a path to recovery. Survivors can learn new, effective ways of regulating the intensity of their feelings, so that they don't need to use alcohol or drugs and/or cut themselves to express their emotions. For many survivors, learning about the psychological impacts of their trauma or abuse helps them to understand why they have struggled for so long, and how they can move forward.

Acknowledging these feelings, understanding where they come from and why they are so intense is an important part of any survivor's journey.

Effects on relationships with others and self-esteem
Survivors often find it difficult to trust others. As children they might have been betrayed by the very adults who were meant to nurture and protect them. As a result, survivors often find it difficult to form and sustain relationships. A large survey of adult survivors

of child abuse in Australia found that survivors had a higher rate of failed relationships and marriages, and reported lower levels of social interaction (Draper, Pirkis et al. 2008).

When children are abused they come to believe the messages their abusers deliver, such as: *'You are worthless'* and *'You have no value'*. Of course, these messages are not true, but children accept and internalise them. These messages become ingrained that, when a child who has been abused or traumatised grows up, the adult survivor will often experience feelings of low self-worth or poor self-confidence. Rebuilding self-esteem is a gradual process, but a crucial one.

Three

A New Identity

Therefore, if anyone is in Christ, he is a new creation; old things have passed away; behold, all things have become new. (2 Corinthians 5:17)

We set a wedding date for the fall of 1977. Wedding plans got underway, and we were married. Yay!

After our wedding we continued to live and work in Calgary. Nana lived with us for another six months or so.

The thought and reality of being married thrilled me. I was sincerely and truly smitten with this man, whom I wanted to spend the rest of my life with. I loved him, but the sexual act of marriage was difficult for me. It repulsed me at times and seemed repugnant and ugly. I was having flashbacks of the sexual trauma that I endured continually as a child.

How would I get through this, work through this? I kept having nightmares or severe flashbacks after sharing an intimate moment with him. It finally got to the point that I had to tell

Allan what was happening to me. I didn't know what else to do; I certainly didn't want to lose him, but I knew I had to be honest with him about what was happening to me emotionally when we cuddled.

Amazingly, Allan understood. He took his time and talked to me about how he was feeling and how he wanted to just hold me. As time went on I started to relax more as we got more intimate with each other. Our passion for one another grew as it should when a couple loves each other with a pure heart as God intended.

So life went on. We had now been married for about three years, going to work, spending time with family, loving each other.

My appetite started to change. I was hungry all the time; I had an appetite like a horse. I have never been a big eater, but I ate more often. I couldn't figure out why, so I decided I had better see my family doctor. He ran some tests and found out that my husband and I were expecting our first child.

I was thrilled. But I cried. How could this be? Considering all the trauma and abuse my body had endured as a child, I never imagined that I would ever be able to become pregnant. Nevertheless, and in spite of my expectations, for the most part my pregnancy was normal.

Four months in, it became medically necessary for me to use a wheelchair more as the paralysis in my right leg was definitely affecting my balance. Would this disability get in the way of me carrying my baby to full term safely?

I was unable to have a normal delivery, and my son Kendel was born through C-section in the winter of 1980. Holding him in my arms after his birth was one of the happiest moments in my life next to getting married.

I loved my son dearly, yet there were moments when I knew that because of my childhood trauma I couldn't show my son how *much* I loved him. My early existence was so perverted! I wasn't able to cuddle him as I needed to or wanted to as his mother, as expressing my love for him in that way seemed foreign and conflicting.

As best as I knew how, I gave my precious son all the love my heart held for him. However, often there were reservations. My history with my parents offered only distorted and dysfunctional parental interaction. In spite of the chaotic and pitiful family history, my mothering instincts kicked in, but with many limitations. There were still daily struggles in caring for my baby boy the way that every child deserves and needs.

I gradually adjusted to being a mom. It wasn't easy— changing his diapers, feeding him, burping him, even wondering as he slept if all was well. And then there was playtime; was I doing that well? I was really unsure how to play with my baby boy. I gradually learned to play baby games with him like patty-cake, this little piggy goes to market, and peekaboo. It felt a little strange at first, but as time went on I slowly started to feel more comfortable in the parent–child interaction.

There were many times when I was second-guessed myself. I learned to ask either my family doctor or a trusted relative about any concerns related to being a mom. I learned as time went on that I could trust the answers that my sisters-in-law gave me.

As the days turned into weeks and the weeks turned into months, my baby boy continued to grow into a healthy and strong little guy. It was a year of firsts for Kendel, from his first words to learning to walk, which thrilled me to pieces.

He helped his dad and me decorate the Christmas tree that year. He was saying a few words already at this point. It's funny how moms are able to understand their babies' first words and baby talk.

Time went on, and we would soon be celebrating our Kendel's first birthday. I tried to make my son's birthday a very happy one for him. Allan had no problem with the plans, but I struggled with the idea of a birthday celebration. We decided to invite mostly family, and it did turn out to be a fun day for Kendel and for everyone else. In the midst of this happiness the disappointments that I had experienced on my childhood birthdays flashed before me. But in spite of my childhood history I learned how to celebrate birthdays and people.

Allan completed his studies and graduated as a journeyman licensed mechanic, and I decided that I wanted to go back to work. I was feeling somewhat restless. I loved being a mom, but there were times when I felt that I needed something more.

I found a job as a receptionist. After about a year I started to grow very tired. I wasn't quite sure why. Again I went in to see my doctor, and I was really surprised to find out that I was expecting again.

This pregnancy was a little more difficult, with bouts of nausea. I had some morning sickness and was very relieved when it stopped. Nine months later, in the spring of 1982, I gave birth to a precious baby girl. She was delivered also by C-section, and Allan and I named her Christine.

Now we had two children. I felt like my life was complete with my husband, whom I loved with all my heart, and our two children, who were gifts from God.

Christine was about two months old when we received word that the place we were renting was being sold and all renters would be required to find alternate accommodation within thirty days. We felt like the rug had been pulled from under us. Allan was without work, and we had no money for a damage deposit in some new location. Social Services suggested that, since Allan couldn't find employment to support us properly, we split up as a family in order for me to receive income support for living and the care of our children. In our desperation, we submitted to this idea with heavy hearts. For almost six months Allan kept away from our little family, all in order to appease Social Services for our financial covering. Thinking of this now, it seems bizarre! When he was finally working full time, we were reunited as a couple and as a family.

Life was returning to normal. My husband went to work every day, and I was a stay-at-home mom with our two children. Kendel and Christine were healthy and continued to grow and learn new things every day. Christine had her year of firsts as well, from birthday to Christmas. I tried to make these occasions special time for my family.

For a while I felt content. Gradually I started to get a feeling of restlessness. I told Allan about how I was feeling and that I thought we needed to move again. We talked it over and after few months decided to move to Red Deer, Alberta. Allan had family living there, and he would be able to find work. So in the spring of 1983 we made the move. He found work immediately, and we stayed with his sister June and her family for a couple of weeks until we settled into our two-bedroom apartment.

We lived in that apartment for about two years. Then Allan and I received word that the building was being turned into an adult condominium, and people with small children would be required to move.

We were able to find a half-duplex to rent that was close to an elementary school. Our son Kendel was turning six and would soon be starting school. So once again I was busy setting up a new place.

Everything was going well for a while. Then the nightmares of the abuse that I experienced as a child started to plague me again. I hated the way the nightmares made me feel. I did my best to push those feelings as far back into my brain as possible so as not to think about them. I forced myself to focus on being a good mother to my children, giving them the best possible care that I could, as well as being there for my husband when he needed me. It worked for a while, as I continued to stay busy with my family and a couple of hobbies.

Then I started to experience difficulties with my son. I had always had some challenges with him even as a little boy because of my own issues from my childhood. So I tried to be careful and use wisdom when it came to disciplining Kendel, but now it was getting worse. I wasn't sure if it was my fault or if my son was just trying to push his boundaries, as all children will do. My husband was away a lot with his work, therefore it was solely up to me much of the time to deal with my son's behaviours, leaving me rather frazzled. I felt drained, believing the problem was always my fault, because I thought that I didn't know how to deal with little children effectively.

It was during this time that I started to think about going to church again. It had been a few years since we as a family had gone to Sunday services. For a number of years I simply had no desire to go to church. I knew God existed, but that's as far as it went. Our children were getting a little older, so Allan and I spoke with his sister, who suggested that we try the church that she and her family attended. This we did.

It felt good to my spirit to go to church again—until the pastor or guest speaker would give a message that included a reference to child sexual abuse. Then those old ugly feelings that I thought I had stuffed far down inside my gut came flooding to the surface. As I listened to the message the terror of the abuse that I experienced as a child would hit my guts with such force internally that at times I just sat there shaking. I couldn't speak or even move in my seat. Other times I would leave the chapel and go to the washroom and just weep. How could I tell anyone that I was a survivor of childhood sexual abuse? There were feelings of being so dirty and empty inside that I could not get away from them, no matter how hard I tried. I would just weep in agony, deep and raw in my spirit, and hopeless futility.

For a few years I continued to go to church, putting a smile on my face as though nothing was wrong and living as normal a life as I possibly could, but I knew I still had this awful secret.

Symptoms of the past abuse were intensifying as years came and went.

Then a thought occurred to me: maybe counselling would help. At least I might get some help in dealing with my son's behaviours. So I made a few phone calls, briefly explaining what I was looking for. It wasn't long before I was able to set up an appointment to see a mental health counsellor in the hopes of being able to open up about the abuse that I experienced, as well as addressing my son's troublesome behaviours.

The counsellor was a man, which I didn't think was a positive for my situation, but I thought to myself, *No, I'll give him a chance; these people are professionals in this field of trauma.* The first few appointments were okay. Then my counsellor started to make me feel like it was all my fault that my son wasn't listening to me. Not long after, I stopped going to counselling.

Around this time, my husband was laid off work. Finances were slim for a couple of months. Then Allan's brother Don, who owned a small repair shop in Ponoka, Alberta, about a half-hour drive from where we were living, offered Allan a job, which he accepted immediately.

Allan drove back and forth to work for about a month. Then we decided we needed to move there. I thought it was a great idea. We moved in the early winter of 1989 to a three-bedroom rental house, and Allan's siblings helped us to move.

THE LONG-TERM EFFECTS
OF CHILD SEXUAL ABUSE
(Child Family Community Australia, CFCA Paper
no. 11, January 2013, accessed March 30, 2016,
https://aifs.gov.au/cfca/publications/long-term-effects-
child-sexual-abuse/interpersonal-outcomes)

There is increasing evidence that children who have
been abused, and in particular sexually abused, have
greater difficulties with interpersonal relationships and
especially trust compared with non-abused individuals.
Given the betrayal of trust and violation of personal
boundaries involved in child sexual victimisation, this
is not surprising. In addition, the secrecy and often
the fear of exposure creates a sense of shame, guilt and
confusion that disrupts the child's "internal working
model" according to which we all interpret the world.
This affects how children and then adults understand
and construe the motives and behaviours of others,
and how they handle stressful life events. Medical and
neurobiological research is throwing new light on the
mechanisms underlying atypical and over-reactive
stress reactions (see below).

Intimate relationships and parenting
There is some evidence for greater difficulties in
interpersonal and particularly intimate relationships
among adults who were sexually abused in childhood.

These include increased instability in relationships, more sexual partners, an increased risk of sexual problems and greater negativity towards partners (Isley, Isley, Freiburger, & McMackin, 2008; Roberts, O'Connor, Dunn, Golding, & ALSPAC Study Team, 2004). Qualitative research including reports from women, indicates that pregnancy, childbirth and motherhood can trigger difficulties, emotional distress and lack of confidence and self-esteem (Sperlich & Seng, 2008). In a large-scale longitudinal prospective study in England, the Avon Longitudinal Study of Parents and Children, Roberts et al. (2004) reported that after adjusting for other childhood adversities, child sexual abuse was associated with "poorer psychological well-being, teenage pregnancy, parenting behaviours, and adjustment problems" (p.525) in their own children. The mothers' anxiety and lack of confidence in parenting mediated the association between child sexual abuse and the perceived quality of their relationships with their own children and their children's adjustment. In a smaller US study, the association between child sexual abuse and parenting outcomes (including parental stress, feelings of competence and discipline strategies) disappeared after accounting for the mother's depression and the current partner's violence (Schuetze & Das Eiden, 2005).

DISRUPTION OF PARENTING
RELATED TO CSA

(Karen A. Duncan, "The Impact of Child Sexual
Abuse on Parenting: A Female Perspective," in
VISTAS: Compelling Perspectives on Counselling, ed.
G. R. Walz and R. K. Yep [Alexandria, VA: American
Counselling Association, 2005], 267-270, accessed
March 30, 2016, https://www.counseling.org/docs/
disaster-and-trauma_sexual-abuse/impact-of-child-
abuse_parenting_female.pdf?sfvrsn=2)

Confusion About Characteristics of Healthy Families

Mothers sexually abused as children report confusion
about healthy family characteristics. This confusion
creates interpersonal conflict which increases internal
stress for the mother and external stress for the child
(Schore, 2001).

The context for this confusion occurred within the
family environment and belief system where a mother
was sexually abused. It then transferred to a mother's
adult life where it influences her thoughts, feelings,
beliefs, and behavior as a mother.

———————————

STRUGGLES WITH SEXUAL INTIMACY
(Barbara Wilson, FamilyLife Canada, accessed March
30, 2016, http://www.familylifecanada.com/2014/09/
why-do-i-struggle/)

In addition to the ways sexual abuse damages our
bodies, spirits and emotions, sexual abuse also damages
our view of sex. When we've been used for others'
sexual pleasure the experience becomes associated with
a negative view of sex...Now something that God
designed for a holy, precious union between a husband
and a wife has been seared on the young person's brain
as something shameful, dirty, and painful.

Then they get married to the person of their dreams.
They're madly in love. They want to have sex with this
person; except, when their sexual desire is aroused,
the unexpected happens. The old familiar feelings
of shame, disgust and the sense that this is wrong
squelches their desire and causes them to shrink back
from the loving touch of their spouse. Or if their abuse
was violent causing fear and feelings of helplessness,
those same emotions will arise during sexual intimacy,
even though this is a safe person. You see, **sexual abuse
not only robs a child of their childhood, but also
steals from their future.** The result is an emotional
and physical withdrawal on the part of the sexual
abuse victim fracturing the marriage union at its
foundation...Healing is a journey, a process. It doesn't

happen overnight...God can heal anyone. He can heal anything. He's done it for me, and countless others. And He wants to do it for you.

Four

LETTING GO OF THE SECRET

"And you shall know the truth, and the truth shall make you free." (John 8:32)

Little did I know that this move would trigger a landslide of emotions and nightmares that could not be stopped. It was like the floodgates broke and nothing was going to stop the flashbacks that were coming forward.

For the first few months after we moved to our new place, I tried not to say anything to anyone about what I was experiencing, because of the intense shame that came with the nightmares and how difficult it was to share this awful secret.

Then I got thinking about the fact that it had been a while since my family and I had gone to church, so I made a few phone calls and found a church that I hoped would be healing for my spirit. My family and I attended for a time; then I started to feel deep within me that I needed some serious help, maybe some sort of counselling.

I made some phones calls and soon found a mental health office in town that was hiring a new counsellor in September, and I was able to make an appointment. Boy, was I relieved when my appointment date finally arrived! It felt like an eternity just waiting. As I was preparing emotionally to see this new counsellor I prayed that the counsellor would be a woman and that she would believe me when I told her that I had been abused. Then I prayed that the counsellor would really hear me and understand me as I spoke to her about the abuse.

My prayers were answered! I was nervous at first. Then I gradually started to feel a sense of relief as I shared with my counsellor, Helen, my secret about what I experienced as a child. She accepted what I was telling her, and it was like the words of my secret just spilled out. Someone was finally listening to me right in the town where we lived. Thank God!

During these counselling times I had many flashbacks. Not long after I started to meet with her, I felt compelled in my gut to press charges against one of the men responsible for molesting me, Frankie. Daddy was always the instigator, God forgive him, but Frankie's expression of the abuse was the most profound, the ugliest.

Daddy and Frankie had an insatiable appetite when it came to molesting me. I remember a few times that having an out-of-body experience in the midst of them savagely molesting me. When my brain couldn't comprehend what Daddy and Frankie were doing to me, my spirit left my body and floated above the bed, watching what they were doing to my body. I couldn't feel anything. I would wake up hours later when the molestation was over and realize that something bad had happened again.

You're probably wondering at this point, where was this child's mother? At these times Mom was away, often for a few hours; more often than not she was away for the whole day. She didn't have the mothering instincts to protect me, and she turned a blind eye to the abuse. Nana said that Mom was rebellious from the get-go. I remember many times—I must have been three or four years old—when Mommy was getting her coat on to go out, I ran to her in desperation, grabbing her skirt hem, crying, begging, and pleading for her not to go bye-bye, because Daddy was going to hurt me again. I remember those words I cried out to Mommy. Mommy angrily peeled my fingers from the bottom of her skirt, yelling at Daddy to come and grab this kid. "She won't let me get out the door." Daddy grabbed me around the waist and held on to me. I would still be crying and screaming for Mommy not to go, and every time I cried out that Daddy was going to hurt me again, he'd put his hand over my mouth to keep me quiet.

Daddy's Lover

I'm Daddy's lover,
He comes creeping into my bed at night,
He holds me close, his arms around me,
He tells me he loves me, his kisses burn.

He starts to caress me, his fingers play tricks,
He starts to undress me, his love I yearn.
I hate him, I hate him,
But I ache for his touch.
I don't like this secret, it hurts too much.

He continues to play, I must confess,
This time together makes me feel a mess.
He's undressed me,
He's on top of me,
His desires grow,
His hands are all over me,
I hate him so.

He's a beast, he's a lover,
He's my daddy so
I can't fight him, I can't beat him,
So I just let go.

I travel to places unknown, the skies are the limit,
My body is frozen, but I'm not in it.
He does what he wants, I can't feel a thing,
His addiction for sex and his evil desires
Leave me cold and alone until he's finished.

I roll over in a heap, he's had his pleasure
I hate this game, I'll hate it forever.

I've tried to tell, and tell I will,
Sexual abuse kills our children,
Kills their will and their spirit.

We *must* take a *stand* and *protect* our children,
Or lose them forever in this secret world
Of sexual abuse.

I remember many times, I was about five years old—I wasn't going to school yet—Daddy watched out the window to make sure that Mommy had gone. Then he grabbed me and cruelly subdued me. I gradually stopped crying, screaming, and kicking. I closed my eyes, and I emotionally disappeared. Daddy was raping me again, and the pain was excruciating— he was tearing me apart. I woke up hours later. My cheeks were wet from tears, and I knew that Daddy had hurt me again. That's when I forced myself to stop remembering just how badly Daddy was hurting me. His actions were incomprehensible. You're probably wondering how a child remembers such trauma. Our human spirits know and remember the truth even when the trauma is so bad that we blank it from our memory. My body and my mind blocked out the worst of the abuse in order to survive the trauma and the betrayal, but over time I started to remember.

I informed Helen of my decision to press charges, and she counselled me as best she could in preparation for the legal journey ahead. She told me several times that it was a very brave step for me to be taking. I sure didn't feel brave. I felt terrified, but I knew in my gut I had to somehow stop these beasts that kept haunting me.

You may be wondering if I had ever tried to press charges against my father for his actions. Yes, I had, a couple of years previously, with my limited resources and understanding, but nothing came of it. Mom and Dad were both questioned. They both called me a liar and said I was making the whole thing up to cause trouble for the family and to tear the family apart. I felt crushed. It's no wonder that survivors of sexual abuse don't come forward.

A Shadow in the Night

I am a shadow in the night.
I come to satisfy your evil lusts.
I am a young woman whose
childhood has been destroyed
and betrayed by predators
like you.

I am a shadow in the night.
I am a child in my emotions,
frozen in time, by predators
like you.
You groomed me in my
actions, you taught me not
to speak. Your secret is safe with me.

I am a shadow in the night.
You stole my innocence,
you tried to kill my spirit.
You threatened me with death,
just to satisfy your evil desires.

I am a shadow in the night.
I walk the streets looking for love.
My heart is dead, my body
full of drugs, just to stop the pain.
I am a shadow in the night.

I am amazed that I even dared to pursue truth in this situation again, now from this different angle. Somehow I had a quiet determination. I had to let the truth of this secret out, no matter what it took.

I wasn't even sure if Frankie was alive, as I had been told years earlier that he had been killed in a car accident. But a couple of days after Christmas that year I got a phone call from the Royal Canadian Mounted Police (RCMP) in Manitoba advising me that Frankie was very much alive and had a recorded history of molesting children. Can you imagine! The officer told me that I would be receiving documents letting me know the court date, which would be in Manitoba. As I was hanging up the phone, I shook in disbelief. Frankie was alive! How could this be? I felt like I was that child again, about to experience the horrific trauma that I had tried so desperately to forget.

The next time I met with Helen, I told her about the phone call from the RCMP. We continued to meet weekly as the real emotional work started. I had been carrying this secret for so long that for me to share even the tiniest bit about the attacks was a terrifying experience.

It took a year of intense counselling to work through the trauma that my emotions had stuffed down for so long and to prepare myself to see this particular man responsible for molesting me. This issue was always in the forefront of my mind, no matter what activity I was engaged in.

Life had to go on. Allan and I decided that we wanted to buy our own place, so he took on a second job, driving on the weekends. It wasn't long before we had saved enough money to put a down payment on our first home. We were thrilled. We made an appointment to meet with a realtor to talk about the style and price of house we were interested in, and shortly after that we found a place we really liked. We wanted everything on one level, as I continued to have trouble with stairs because of my disability, and we found a mobile home.

Our moving plans gradually came into place. We were in the process of packing to get ready for this move when I received the documents stating that I needed to go to court in Manitoba. This huge secret was soon to be exposed publicly before the courts!

Allan and I moved into our new home, and in the next couple of weeks we'd be going to Winnipeg for court. Again in the forefront of my mind, the thought of seeing this man again made me feel anxious and at times physically sick to my stomach.

Do I really have to do this? Am I doing the right thing? I must! But my father got away scot free. Am I going to get slapped in the face again? I hated the very thought of entering into this process. But I knew in my gut I had to see this through to the end. I could not let another man get away with this molestation. I had to let this awful secret out, no matter how scared I felt, and, believe me, I was terrified. I had been threatened many times by Daddy and Frankie that if I ever told this secret to anyone, I would be killed or a member of my family would be injured. That's how child molesters get away with their devious crimes.

As the court date quickly approached, Allan and I made arrangements for our children to stay with an aunt and uncle, as I didn't feel it was safe to have them with us on this trip. Once all the arrangements were taken care of, it wasn't long before we were on the road to Manitoba. As soon as we arrived in Manitoba, I connected with the court, as I needed to go over a few details with Victim Services.

The court meeting was here! Seeing Frankie the molester in court was horrific, and being questioned by his lawyer and then by the judge was even worse. Frankie's lawyer tried to discredit my memory in the hope that I wouldn't remember certain details about Frankie's appearance when he was molesting me so many years before. When a child is molested by the same person repeatedly over a period of time, she can't forget his face, hair colour and length, smell, or voice. I knew the moment that Frankie walked into the courtroom that it was him, and my gut jumped in terror the second I recognized him. I felt like I was that child again, being raped one more time. It was the hardest thing I've ever had to do, and when the court procedure was over, I sat in my chair and wept. I was drained emotionally; I was numb. What a piece of hell on earth for me.

Following the court proceedings Allan and I visited my sister, her husband, and their children, who lived in the city. It had been years since I had seen my sister last, only connecting occasionally through letters. It was great to see them again even for this brief visit. But finally we were on the road again, heading back to Alberta, and I was extremely glad to be going home.

By the time we left Winnipeg, the court determination had been finalized. Frankie walked away with a smug smile. He had again conned the justice system and was walking away free! I experienced betrayal by the system again. This perpetrator had a known history of molesting children, yet his lawyer was able to explain away the case before the court. His changed appearance over the years from when the attacks first happened until I was an adult facing him in court was enough to dismiss the matter. He again was a free man!

A couple of months later, my counsellor informed me that she had received a transfer to Calgary. So we got together one more time to say our goodbyes.

About six months after this court process, depression started to affect me. I wasn't sure what was happening to me. At times I felt an intense sadness; at other times I felt really angry at the results of the court determination. Frankie simply got probation for his horrific molestation of a little girl.

I decided I needed to phone the mental health office to find out if I could see another counsellor to help me work through the feelings I was experiencing from the aftermath of the court process. They suggested that I take anti-depression medication for a while to see if it would ease some of the symptoms. The medicine did help for quite some time, lifting the depression and putting a lid on the darkness that I had walked through and was continuing to walk through daily. The depression itself was held at bay for the most part, but the emotional root pain still tormented me. This went on for ten years.

Even when I was on this medication there was a sense in me that I was constantly struggling to get out of the deep, dark, endless pit that was swallowing me up. I was still living in a hell.

During this time Allan and I were discussing family, work, and life in general. He had changed jobs a couple of times, mostly due to work lay-offs. We prayed together about whether we should stay where we were or seek employment in another location. After much prayer, and discussion, Allan and I decided we needed to move back to Red Deer. I felt such a draw in my gut for Red Deer that I knew this move was right.

Over the next few weeks we drove into Red Deer numerous times for Allan to drop off his resumes. We prayed in every decision for guidance and that every concern we had would be taken care of. Soon all the arrangements for our move back were made.

Allan made arrangements for our mobile home to be moved to Red Deer, and we planned to stay with family briefly until we could get settled into our new location. I was so happy that at times I could hardly contain my joy. Our children were just as happy that they were coming back to Red Deer, even though they were leaving some of their friends behind. To this date we have stayed in touch with some of the friends that we made in Ponoka.

We moved back to Red Deer in the summer of 1997. It took a couple of months for our family to get familiar with our new community, and our children made friends fairly quickly.

Allan was busy with his new job, and his sister June and her husband helped us to get settled into our new place. By September our daughter Christine was getting ready to go back to school and our son Kendel was looking for work. It definitely was a busy year for my family as we settled into our new place.

My nana passed away in the spring of 1998. That was a new beginning for me, as Nana was my rock. It took a few years to get over the shock that Nana was actually gone and that I couldn't talk to her anymore about daily happenings or to hear her voice on the phone. She was the one person I had grown to trust with all my heart. She was everything I needed. Nana was my saviour; she was my stability. I loved her dearly. Without her I felt lost and lonely. That's when I started to cry out to Jesus to help me.

I grew up being taught that Jesus loved me and that He had died on the cross for my sins, but was I truly ready to have Him come into my heart and heal the sorrow of losing Nana as well as the wounds of my childhood that ran so deep for so long? I really didn't know if I would ever get past that secret or if Jesus even cared enough to help me. Was my understanding of Jesus incomplete?

Over the next few years a quiet determination grew in my heart. I knew I had to find out more about who Jesus was and if He really loved me. I was soon to discover just how much Jesus really loves me. "For God so loved the world that He gave His only begotten Son, that whoever believes in Him should not perish but have everlasting life" (John 3:16). But could I trust Him enough to help me look at and heal the secret of my past? That was the key.

Our family started going to church again, and as time went on I realized that I needed more counselling. I knew I was still holding people at arm's length, detaching myself from those around me to hide the secret. I guess that was deep within me, yet unresolved and unhealed. I still felt so filthy.

VICTIM RIGHTS IN CANADA
(Canadian Resource Centre for Victims of Crime, accessed March 30, 2016, http://crcvc.ca/for-victims/rights/)

RIGHTS
The Canadian Victims Bill of Rights
Enacted on July 23rd, 2015, the Act creates clear rights for victims of crime, and requires said rights to be considered during each step of the criminal justice system. The *Canadian Victims Bill of Rights* provides 4 principal rights to victims. These include:

1) Right to information:

- Victims will be able to obtain information about the criminal justice system, as well as available victim services and resources. In addition, victims can receive information about the investigation, sentencing, and prosecution of the person who harmed them.
- Victims who have registered with the Parole Board of Canada or Correctional Service Canada can access information about the offender who harmed them including: release dates, progress updates, conditions that may affect them and copies of Parole Board decisions.

2) Right to protection:

- Victims will have the right to have their security, identity, and privacy protected. Victims will also be protected from retaliation and intimidation.
- When testifying in court, victims will have the right to request testimonial aids such as: assistance from a support person, testifying by video (CCTV), or testifying from behind a screen.

3) Right to participation:

- Victims have the right to prepare and deliver Victim Impact Statements.
- Victims have the right to express their views about the court's decisions that affect their rights.

4) Right to seek restitution:

- Courts must consider restitution to the victim in all cases. Victims have the opportunity to describe and claim financial losses. Judges can order restitution for a number of reasons including: psychological harm, physical harm, temporary housing/childcare costs, and identity theft.

REMEDIES for breaches of rights:

When a victim believes that his or her rights have been breached, the victim would first file a complaint with the appropriate federal department or agency. The legislation includes a requirement for all federal departments and agencies that have responsibilities under the *Canadian Victims Bill of Rights* to have internal complaint mechanisms accessible to victims that would review complaints, make recommendations to correct any infringement, and notify victims about the results of the review. Complaints regarding a provincial or territorial agency, including police, Crown, or victim services, would be addressed in accordance with the applicable provincial or territorial legislation.

Five

ACCEPTING THE TRUTH

*He heals the brokenhearted And binds up their wounds.
He counts the number of the stars; He calls them all
by name. Great is our Lord, and mighty in power; His
understanding is infinite.* (Psalm 147:3–5)

In 2002 I met with Janie, a Christian prayer counsellor. Before
we got into a discussion about why I was there she asked
if we could pray. I felt her respect for me. As I started to tell
her the secret of my past, peace started to come over me. But
could I truly trust her—or this Jesus that she represented, for
that matter—to help me get rid of the garbage? Yet there was
something supernatural going on. Jesus brought me here.

The trust between my counsellor and me started to grow,
as did my trust in this Jesus that she represented. Historically,
trusting has not been easy for me, from family experience to
court experience and even mental health personnel interaction,
so we met week by week, always a matter of baby steps. And

"baby steps" is not an exaggeration, because my wounding was from infancy on.

When a child is abused as an infant, his or her trust is grossly destroyed. The behaviour the child is groomed into seems normal, until that child sees other parent–child interactions and then questions his or her own understanding and upbringing. Even simple adult–child interactions were confusing to me. I couldn't understand innocent interactions in this area. A touch on a child's shoulder by an adult would raise a red flag to me: *Something is very wrong here.*

It has taken me a very long time, most of my life, to get to this point of healing, to know I can truly trust in the triune God, to know and feel with every fibre of my being that God really does love me and that He is guiding my steps. I have also learned and know that God is very loving and forgiving. I have been learning to give him the problem, even when I am the one who has messed up.

When we started to investigate my past in counselling, the lights were turning on. Triggers were exposing the darkness of my childhood abuse. As we continued to meet weekly to expose the trauma and the things of darkness that I was not totally cognizant of at the time, we experienced an amazing outpouring of God as we worked through the garbage of my sordid and distorted past. We soon discovered that I had many fragmented parts, which were cautiously coming to the light to be heard and acknowledged. Their stories varied in personality and function. They wanted to be heard; they were no longer to be silenced. One would display verbally through me a fearfulness, a timidity, like a very young child; another, a powerful and provocative older child; another, a silent presence of perhaps one hiding; another, a permissive expression. And the list goes on. These parts often had names for themselves.

Something was different in this counselling encounter. There was a quiet presence in the room, a presence that felt safe. I could share each story without feeling threatened. I didn't understand that presence at first. There was a purity about it that I had not experienced before. The fragmented parts of me slowly started to experience healing, and I gradually sensed a glimmer of hope that this dark journey I had been on for so long was gradually coming to an end.

My counselor says that the Holy Spirit led and directed our sessions towards healing of all these soul wounds that displayed their various expressions of emotional pain and coping. Really, this experience is a mystery that only God can explain. It was almost too much for me to fathom, or to even imagine, that every struggle that I had ever experienced, endured, and lived through would gradually be corrected. The toxic parental care would be exposed for what it was, and I was no longer a victim on this journey of hope.

In 2003 Allan and I were invited to attend a Bible study. This Bible study gave me a better understanding of Scriptures, and I learned more about Jesus. At the end of the Bible study course, the facilitator asked if there was anyone in the group that would like to invite Jesus into their heart. I was so excited that I could hardly wait for the facilitator to finish with the invitation. I put my hand up right away. I actually surprised myself. I knew in my heart that I was ready to publicly express that I wanted Jesus to rule and reign in my life. Shortly after the Bible study group was finished, Pat and Rita and I started to meet on a regular basis for more spiritual counselling. That was a two-year journey of healing.

RECOMMENDED BOOKS ON
SPIRITUAL COUNSELLING

Paula Sandford, *Garlands for Ashes: Healing Victims of Sexual Abuse* (Tulsa, Oklahoma: Victory House, 1988).

Paula Sandford, *Healing Victims of Sexual Abuse* (Florida: Charisma House, 2009).

John Sandford and Paula Sandford, *Healing the Wounded Spirit* (Victory House, 1985).

Mark Virkler and Patti Virkler, *Counselled by God* (Belleville, Ontario: Essence Publishing, 2003).

Six

LEARNING TO TRUST

Trust in the Lord with all your heart. Never rely on what you think you know. Remember the Lord in everything you do, and he will show you the right way. (Proverbs 3:5–6 GNT)

L earning to trust has not been an easy task for me. It will take a lifetime of learning. There are still moments when I experience panic and terror and wonder if I will ever be totally free of this secret and its many little pockets. I am learning to trust in Jesus at a deeper level. I am learning to listen more with my gut. As a victim of childhood sexual abuse I was groomed to behave a certain way and to trust certain people regardless of how many times they betrayed me. Now through Bible study and spiritual counselling, I am learning to trust in Jesus, one task at a time.

Over the years, I have been to numerous doctors, secular counsellors, psychiatrists, mental health professionals, and even Christian pastors, all in hope of them helping me find the truth about my childhood. I was having nightmares; were they flashbacks of trauma that was not being resolved?

I recall at a very young age—I must have been five or six years old—sitting in the middle of my parents' living room floor, thinking to myself that if I ever grew up, if I ever got married, if I ever had children, my children would never, ever experience the hell that I lived through on a daily basis. My childhood was a nightmare. I had very few, if any, happy and safe moments. My daily experience from infancy was extreme neglect and extreme abuse of all kinds, more than the average mind can comprehend. The trauma that I lived through was unconscionable.

My counsellor gave me Scripture verses from the Bible each week that I was to read aloud to myself and memorize. "For the word of God is living and powerful, and sharper than any two-edged sword, piercing even to the division of soul and spirit, and of joints and marrow, and is a discerner of the thoughts and intents of the heart" (Hebrews 4:12). "He heals the brokenhearted And binds up their wounds. He counts the number of the stars; He calls them all by name. Great is our Lord, and mighty in power; His understanding is infinite" (Psalm 147:3-5). The Word of God is miraculous when received by faith.

As my counselling with Janie drew to a close, about two years after we first met, I finally accepted that I could now move forward with my life. I had experienced so much of Jesus. I had experienced a sense of peace and a sense of belonging that only comes from knowing Him. I experienced His interception and power to transform a shattered past. It is still a very slow journey at times as I continue to pray daily for guidance and read the Bible and trust in Jesus.

During this long and challenging experience, God has given me spiritual tools to work with. My faith in God is growing and being stretched. My trust in Him and in His Word is growing daily. Obedience to His direction is an amazing blessing. To know beyond any human experience a sense of power and peace that only comes from God is mind boggling. When I'm going in the right direction, He confirms. And likewise when I have been headed in the wrong direction, I have a very strong sense of going in the wrong direction. Amazing!

In 2005, after months of praying, I decided I needed to be baptized. I had been thinking about baptism, immersion, for well over a year, and the daily reading of God's Word had been gently guiding me through that time. "Go therefore and make disciples of all the nations, baptizing them in the name of the Father and of the Son and of the Holy Spirit" (Matthew 28:19). "Repent, and let every one of you be baptized" (Acts 2:38). I did it—I got baptized.

It has not been an easy journey, but I have come to know and sense when God is guiding me. A few months after getting baptized God impressed upon my heart that I should join another church congregation. That too was not an easy decision for me to make. I liked the church I was attending and had made friends, but I knew I had to obey what I was being asked to do in my heart.

I Am a Child of the Night

I am a child, I am a child
I walk the streets looking for love,
I've been betrayed by the man,
The father I love.

I stand on the street corner,
Waiting and cold,
My spirit is dead,
I'm hungry and old
I need to turn a trick,
Before my spirit feels the pain.

Oh, here comes my lover,
I don't know his name.
I get in his car, and off I go again.
To places unknown, a secret to most.
Down back alleys and tunnels
that thrive in the dark.

I give him what he wants,
Or he'll take it from me,
I hate this, I hate this

I don't like what I see.
I feel used and abandoned
I feel there's nothing better for me.

I go back to my corner,
And there I wait,
For the next Joe to come
And start all over again.

This life on the street is
A cycle of horror,
For children like me,
Who turn tricks to survive.
The needle I use, one more time,
Though I hate.
I'm a child, I'm a child,
A child of the night.

———————————————

DEALING WITH NIGHTMARES
AND FLASHBACKS
(Sexual Assault Resource Centre, accessed March 30, 2016, http://www.kemh.health.wa.gov.au/services/sarc/documents/flashback.pdf)

Many people seek counselling for sexual assault or sexual abuse because they are experiencing constant reminders of the event in the form of flashbacks and nightmares. These reminders can be incredibly intrusive and can contribute to the development of anxiety problems, sleep disturbance and feelings of being out of control. Some feel that they are going crazy. Some believe they should not be affected so greatly by the assault or abuse.

Important things to remember:
- Sexual assault is a traumatic event
- People who have experienced a traumatic event often experience flashbacks and nightmares
- You are not going crazy
- There are some things you can do that can help you manage these reminders of the trauma

Flashbacks
- Flashbacks occur when we are triggered to remember what has happened. A flashback can be a terribly frightening experience, involving all of the senses. Many people say that they can see,

hear, smell and feel everything that happened to them during a flashback. Some people feel as if they are reliving the trauma.

- Identifying your triggers can help you to know why a flashback may occur.

- A trigger is something that causes us to subconsciously switch into a flashback. It can be something like seeing someone who looks like the assailant, hearing a word or a phrase that reminds you of the assault or abuse, driving past the area where the assault or abuse took place, birthdays or anniversaries, childbirth, or television shows. It can be anything. People have their own trigger or triggers that are unique to them.

- Sometimes new memories or things that don't quite make sense may surface in a flashback. This means that your mind is still processing the trauma and trying to make sense of things. Human memory is not like a computer memory where things are straightforward and in a line, it is interwoven with emotion, thoughts and experiences.

- 'Grounding' is a tool that people use to help manage flashbacks. It is used to help you remain in the here and now and not feel like you are reliving the trauma.

Some people carry an item that they can grab hold of if they are feeling like they may be triggered, such as a piece of jewellery or a rock. Others remind themselves where they are by looking around and saying what they see.

- It is important that you remind yourself that you are safe and that you are not reliving the trauma, no matter how bad it feels.
- After the flashback is over, try to understand it. Perhaps write it down or talk about it with a trusted friend or a counsellor
- Sometimes it is helpful to rate the flashback, with, for example 10 being the worst, 0 being the best. It can help you get an idea of how things are going for you over time...

Nightmares

- A lot of people experience nightmares. The nightmare can be a replay of the trauma or may be quite bizarre and seemingly unrelated.
- Sometimes writing the dream down can help you to make sense of it. Also writing it down and then changing the ending, giving yourself a positive outcome and reading the new ending before you go to sleep at night may change the content of the dream (you may need to do this a few times).
- Try drawing or painting the nightmare. It doesn't have to be a masterpiece.

- Creative visualisation can help. Visualise yourself having a refreshing night's sleep or having a protective barrier around yourself or your door. Visualise a different ending to your dream.
- Talk about your dreams with a trusted friend or counsellor. Talking can make you feel your dreams have less control over you.
- Try to understand why you are having nightmares. Nightmares can occur as a result of triggers. If you have not had nightmares for a while or they are getting worse, there could be something happening in your life that may be triggering these nightmares.

Seven

CLOSURE OF MY PAST

Heal me, O LORD, and I shall be healed; Save me, and
I shall be saved, For You are my praise. (Jeremiah 17:14)

In 2006 I received a call from my cousin, inviting me to a
family reunion the following summer in Manitoba. Without
hesitation I said yes. I really wasn't sure why I said yes; normally
I would have said no. I didn't fight the thought of going to
Manitoba, though. I just knew in my gut that my husband and
I would go. Besides, it had been a few years since I had seen my
sister and her family. I didn't know at the time that I would be
seeing my mother shortly after the reunion ended.

Allan and I planned to take an extra day to do some
sightseeing in Manitoba. However, on Monday my sister, Lee,
got a call from her daughter, Ashley, who had been asked by
the court to be the liaison regarding Mom's affairs. Apparently
Mom was in a crisis situation related to her residence, causing
her to be evicted yet again. This, I later learned, had been her

pattern for a number of years. Keep in mind that Lee and I had had very little contact with each other or our mother over the previous decade. I felt compelled to check into Mom's situation before returning to Alberta.

I didn't know the reason for the eviction, so I made a few phone calls and tracked down where Mom was being cared for. I was able to talk with the agency counsellor overseeing her care, who told me that Mom was in the process of being assessed for future care. She gave me the address of where Mom was staying, and soon Allan and I arrived there.

After we talked with her counsellor for a few minutes, she asked if Allan and I wanted to wait in the cafeteria while she went to get Mom from her room. We didn't have to wait for long. The cafeteria door opened, and there she was.

Mom came into the room, using her walker for stability. Her counsellor followed a couple of steps behind. I almost didn't recognize her. Mom had aged considerably since the last time I had seen her, at my dear nana's funeral in May 1998. I felt very nervous about seeing her again, but I was also concerned about her current state of affairs and the fact that she was in this compromised situation.

She stood for a moment just looking at me, our eyes connecting briefly. Then Mom opened her arms to me, and I walked into her embrace. For the first time in years I felt Mommy's arms around me and heard her tell me that she loved me. I stood in her embrace, and the tears flowed.

I felt like I was that little girl again. The broken promises, the betrayal, and all the disappointments slowly vanished. I accepted Mommy for who she was and the love she was able to give me in that moment.

Mom's counsellor invited Allan and me to join Mom for supper that evening, and we accepted. It allowed me the opportunity to have a short visit with Mom and to determine that she was getting good care. We were subsequently invited to visit her a couple more times before we returned home to Alberta. I'm glad that bravery trumped fear and that I took the time to visit her even though I was terrified at the time.

When I look back on that moment in time with my mom, I consider it a gift from God. I experienced peace and closure in my spirit. But if God hadn't blessed me with the opportunity to see Mom one more time, I would have been okay. I would still have come away from all this with a basic understanding of her love for me.

Allan and I returned to Alberta and resumed our lives and schedules.

In early March 2008 I received a phone call from my brother in Manitoba, informing me that Dad was in the hospital. He wasn't doing very well. I asked my brother several pertinent questions in regards to Dad's medical status; then I phoned the hospital to confirm the information, as my brother is mentally challenged and at times gets information mixed up.

After I identified myself, Dad's nurse confirmed the information. As I hung up the phone I knew in my gut that I was going back to Manitoba to see Dad. It's not that I *wanted* to go; I knew I *had* to go back to see him.

It took me a couple of days to make the necessary arrangements to fly to Winnipeg. I didn't know what to expect when I got there, but I wasn't going to put up with any garbage as far as Dad's behaviour went. My defences were definitely up.

As the plane was approaching the Winnipeg airport for landing, a thought suddenly hit me: *What am I doing? Mom and Dad never ran after us kids like this, no matter how sick we were. Nana was the one who came to the hospital to see us anytime we were hospitalized, not Mom and Dad.* As the plane landed I gave myself permission to leave if at any time during this visit the situation felt too intense. I was an adult now, and I could make my own decisions.

My niece, Ashley, met me at the airport. I was very glad to see her. She took me directly up to the hospital to see Dad, and my sister met us there. As we got off the elevator, Ashley offered to wait to allow me a few minutes alone with Dad. I felt extremely nervous—*terrified* may be more accurate. I didn't know what to expect and I really didn't want to see him, but I knew I had to. I went to the nurse's station and identified myself, and the staff directed me to him.

He was sleeping when I stepped into his room, and I didn't recognize him. I spoke his name softly, and he opened his eyes. Dad had certainly aged in the twenty-plus years since I had seen him last. Life had taken a toll on him.

I slowly approached his bed. I was terrified, like I was that little vulnerable girl again. As he reached his hands toward me, he looked frail, not the child molester I remembered. Yet in that moment all I felt was terror. I told myself, *Just breathe, breathe. It's okay.*

I cautiously took Dad's frail hands in mine, thinking, *Take it slow and be careful.* I held those frail hands for a few minutes as tears gently ran down my cheeks. Something took over—amazing grace.

Dad was surprised to see me. In a weak voice he said he never, ever, expected to see me again after I left Winnipeg so many years before. Our conversation was short. He complained about his medical situation, and my internal response was one of disdain because he was so self-focused, as if he was the only one hurting in that moment. I wondered if he ever stopped to think of the years of abuse that he inflicted on my siblings and me without an ounce of remorse.

We chatted for a couple more minutes; then I told him that I would be back to see him in the morning. He tilted his face up, seemingly for me to kiss his lips, which I could not do—I would not do. Instead I leaned his head forward and gently kissed his forehead. I told him that I loved him and that I would indeed be back in the morning. I was amazed at the supernatural kindness that accompanied me in that room.

My brother, sister and I, along with my sister's children, took turns sitting with Dad that week. He lingered for another week before he passed away. We had a small memorial service for him with mainly family and a few close friends. My niece Ashley graciously stepped up and offered to plan the service. A couple of days after Dad's memorial service, I flew back to Alberta.

I'm amazed at God's hand upon this whole situation and that final memorial service. I was required to read my father's eulogy and wasn't tempted to shame his name in any way before those present, veterans and old drinking buddies alike.

I had come to understand from the Lord's Prayer that I cannot receive forgiveness for my failing and sin when I will not forgive those who have sinned against me. Really, it was a miraculous transaction that happened to me. The realization, especially following my water baptism, that Jesus went on the cross for me taught me that extending forgiveness sets me free.

Six months after Daddy's passing, I was relaxing at home one morning when I saw in my spirit all the emotional pain of my past shattering, exploding into a million pieces. I saw a pane of glass, the window in my soul, letting go. I needed to let go of the pain of my past in order to embrace and step into my future. It was a new beginning.

On another occasion I was sitting at my kitchen table, again experiencing a spiritual revelation that only comes from God. I was standing in the sand on a shoreline. The glass windowpane was shattered into a million pieces at my feet. As I watched the ocean water come up to the sandy shore, then wash out and return again, whatever marks were left in the sand were cleared away. The millions of pieces of the shattered windowpane were taken out to sea. A time of healing and renewing was taking place within my spirit.

It has taken me a few years to get past the fact that Daddy's gone, but I've also come to understand that being able to spend that last week with him was a gift from God. The first time ever that I saw my father cry was when I stood in the doorway of his hospital room and he realized that I had come to see him. I loved him very much. I have been able to experience peace, forgiveness, and closure in my spirit because I was able to see him one last time before he passed. It is only by God's grace that I was compelled to go to Manitoba and be with my father those last days and experienced a miracle of forgiveness and closure that only comes from knowing God and experiencing His love.

My Jesus, my Jesus,
I love you so.
Your arms are wide open,
I had no place to go.
You gave me love,
You fixed my broken heart,
You took my old life,
You gave me a fresh start.

You give me direction, from your Word of truth,
I love you, dear Jesus
I love you, I do.

A Welcomed Visitor

Trailer door wide open,
Expecting company,
It's a beautiful spring day.
The air is fresh, there's a gentle breeze
Wafting through the rooms.

The air smells sweet to the nose.
My senses tingle with anticipation,
Waiting for our special guest to arrive.

The doorbell rings, our guest is here.
The air tingles with excitement,
The anticipation is over.
We greet one another with
Warm embraces.
We look forward to a wonderful visit.

The coffee is made,
Refreshments are served.

We each settle in to enjoy the visit.
We exchange stories of
Love, encouragement,
Sadness and joy.

Before we know it,
Our visit comes to a close.
We get up from our places
And prepare to say our farewells.
Our hearts, our spirits, are briefly saddened,
As we know our guest has to leave.

We make plans for the future, our guest to see,
As we bid farewell,
Our hearts saddened temporarily.
We know we will see
Each other again soon,
In our home in heaven,
A more permanent place,
Where there will be
More laughter, more joy
That time can't erase.

So come along, children,
And study real hard
On this journey through life
That has many twists and turns.

God's Word is true,
He will give you direction.
His arms are wide open,
His Love *is* perfection.

So take the time now,
Without further delay,
And ask Jesus to come
Into your heart to stay.

He will guide you,
He will love you,
He will in every way.
This guest we've longed for
Is here to stay.

Welcome home.